POCKET PICTORIAL GUIDE TO

East A

John Potter

MYRIAD

LONDON

Dedham Located on the Essex bank of the river Stour opposite Flatford, the fine village of Dedham has many associations with the painter John Constable. The half-timbered Marlborough Head Hotel (left) is in the town centre.

Flatford Mill This atmospheric spot (below left) where Constable grew up is the subject of many of his most famous paintings.

St Mary the Virgin Dedham's beautiful parish church (below) was a favourite of Constable and often features in his work. The church has one of Constable's few religious paintings, *The Ascension*, hanging in the nave opposite the north porch.

Colchester Colchester Castle is now a museum illustrating the history of the town. Tymperleys Clock Museum (above) is housed in a 15th-century timber-framed building.
Colchester Town Hall's 162ft Victoria Tower (right) dominates the high street. The statue at the top is of St Helena, patron saint of Colchester.

Brightlingsea Lying at the mouth of the river Colne, the lively beach front (left) looks across to Mersea Island.

Maldon The historic hill town of Maldon stands at the head of the Blackwater Estuary. It is home to many beautiful Thames sailing barges which can be seen regularly moored up by The Jolly Sailor Inn at the quay. These historic boats, often known as "haystackers" due to the piles of hay on deck, carried cargo from the farmlands of Essex to the capital.

Tollesbury Often referred to as the village of the "plough and sail", because it relied on the harvest of both the land and sea, Tollesbury Quay (above) has a row of restored wooden sail lofts.

Blackwater Estuary
This estuary is one of a series of beautiful muddy inlets (left) which are typical of the Essex coastline.

Essex Sunshine Coast

The north Essex coastal towns of Clacton, Frinton and Walton share a clean sandy beach which stretches from Colne Point in the south to Walton-on-the Naze; the Naze is a natural headland which protrudes into the North Sea. The famous pier at Clacton (below) was built in the late 1900s and gave large boats from London the ability to moor and unload passengers.

Thaxted Lowe's Mill was built in 1804 by John Webb to feed the growing population of London. The mill now houses an agricultural museum. Thaxted hosts the annual gathering of Morris Men who perform in the town and surrounding villages. The Chantry (bottom) located in the churchyard of St John the Baptist was formerly the priest's accommodation; it is now used as an almshouse.

Finchingfield This picture postcard village (right) is situated between Sible Hedingham and Thaxted on the Braintree to Saffron Walden road. The village has a pretty green, a duckpond, a narrow bridge which straddles the stream and a windmill, together with several medieval houses known as *cabbaches*. Many of the cottages have decorative plaster-work, or "pargeting", on their walls; this is a characteristic feature of buildings in the area.

Aldeburgh The modern sculpture *Scallop*, by artist Maggi Hambling on Aldeburgh beach, is a tribute to the composer Benjamin Britten who made his home in the town.

Snape Maltings The quay along the river Alde at Snape Maltings. The Maltings now host the annual Aldeburgh Music Festival.

Orford This unspoiled fishing and tourist village on the estuary of the river Alde is dominated by the keep of the 12th-century Royal Castle (right). Opposite Orford, on the far side of the river Alde, lies Orford Ness, a long spit stretching 10 miles up the coast to Aldeburgh. A few hundred years ago the estuary of the river was just south of Aldeburgh. Over time silting up of the river mouth diverted its path and created a spit between the river and the sea extending over 10 miles down the coast towards Orford, enclosing the estuaries of both the rivers Alde and Ore. This has created a long stretch of sheltered water which is perfect for sailing and boating.

Southwold Bounded by the North Sea to the east, the river Blyth and Southwold harbour to the south-west and Buss Creek to the north, this elegant seaside town is virtually an island. The tall white tower of the lighthouse is a notable landmark in the centre of the town; constructed in 1887 it replaced three local lighthouses threatened by coastal erosion. The resort has over 300 beautifully painted beach huts which evolved from fishermen's and bathers' huts. The huts are lifted from the beach each autumn by a crane in order to be safe from high tides. In 1872 George and Ernest Adnams bought the Sole Bay Brewery in Southwold and established Adnams, now one of the major businesses in the town. Adnams has many pubs throughout East Anglia and two fine hotels in Southwold, The Swan and The Crown.

Walberswick Just across the river Blyth from Southwold, Walberswick (right) was once a thriving trading port. A ferryboat across the river links the town with Southwold to the north.

Blythburgh Surrounded by beautiful countryside, Blythburgh's magnificent parish church, Holy Trinity (below) known as "The Cathedral of the Marshes" towers over the saltmarshes.

Dunwich Once the capital of East Anglia, Dunwich (left and right) was a major trading, fishing and shipbuilding centre with a population of over 3,000. But like so many other settlements along the East Anglian coast, coastal erosion gradually took its toll and much of the town was lost to the sea. The town once had eight churches; almost all had to be abandoned as the sea advanced inland. It is said that it is sometimes possible to hear the sound of church bells coming up from the depths on quiet nights.

Lavenham The medieval village of Lavenham lies a few miles north-east of Sudbury and is famous for its collection of half-timbered buildings. During the late middle ages it was one of the wealthiest towns in Britain thanks to the prosperity of the local wool trade.

Clare On the north bank of the river Stour, this beautiful market town is dominated by its castle mound which offers panoramic views of the town and the impressive roof and spire of St Peter and St Paul. The mound has remains of the old stone castle keep as well as the former railway track and station – the only rail line in the UK to be built inside castle grounds.

Framlingham The sturdy battlements and 13 towers of Framlingham Castle are a magnificent landmark with views across the mere. It was at Framlingham that Mary Stuart was proclaimed Queen of England following the death of her father, Henry VIII.

Cambridge The famous Baron of Beef pub in Bridge Street lies a short distance from Magdalene Bridge. No visit to Cambridge is complete without a trip in a punt. These traditional flat-bottomed boats were used widely in the Fens, the marshy flat lands to the north of the city. The gardens of Clare College (right) form part of the famous Backs – the rear part of those colleges which border the beautiful river Cam. King's College (below right) was founded in 1441 by Henry VI. Its famous chapel is home to the renowned King's College Choir, whose Christmas Eve service is broadcast around the world.

St Neots The largest town in Cambridgeshire, St Neots is situated on the Great Ouse, which meanders peacefully through the town and forms the border with the historic county of Huntingdonshire. The town was the site of a medieval priory built to house the remains of the Cornish monk Neot. Today the tower of the parish church of St Mary (left) dominates the town centre.

Ely The majestic cathedral (above right) is known locally as "the ship of the Fens" because its slender tower looms above the surrounding flat countryside. The eight-sided tower in the centre of the church is the only Gothic dome in existence and the cathedral is within the walls of a Benedictine monastery.

Sandringham The beautiful country retreat of the Queen and the Duke of Edinburgh has been passed down through four generations of the royal family.

Royal estate West Newton primary school (above) and church (above right) are on the Sandringham estate. HRH the Prince of Wales and the Duchess of Cornwall open the flower show at Sandringham (right). This popular event attracts thousands of visitors to the royal estate each July. The tiny village of Anmer (below) is situated between Sandringham and Houghton Hall.

Anmer Lined with attractive flint and redbrick cottages, this quiet village is part of the royal estate. Surrounded by a canopy of mature trees, the small church of St Mary contains beautiful stained-glass windows; it was a particular favourite of Queen Mary, the wife of George V.

Blickling Hall One of England's finest Jacobean houses, Blickling Hall (right) was once home to Anne Boleyn, the wife of Henry VIII and the mother of Queen Elizabeth I. The house is famous for its long gallery, fine furniture, superb library, pictures and tapestries.

Houghton Hall
Home of Britain's first prime minister, Sir Robert Walpole, this fine mansion with its magnificent stable block is set in 350 acres of fine gardens and parkland. The house features a Toy Soldier Museum.

Norwich The magnificent cathedral of the Holy and Undivided Trinity – known as Norwich Cathedral – dominates the city centre and is the focus of spiritual life in Norfolk. The impressive two-storey cloisters (right) played a key part in the life of the original Benedictine monastery. The castle at Norwich (below left) was originally a wooden motte and bailey construction built by William the Conqueror in 1067. Today the castle serves as the city museum.

Castle Rising The keep at Castle Rising (below) is the most spectacular remnant of the massive stone defensive castle built by William d'Aubigny to celebrate his marriage to the widow of Henry I.

Castle Acre The peaceful village of Castle Acre a few miles north of Swaffham is famous for the twin ruins of Castle Acre castle (right) which stands close to the village and Castle Acre priory (below) which is a short distance to the south.

Holkham Hall This beautiful 18th century Palladian-style mansion was built between 1734 and 1762 for Thomas Coke, first Earl of Leicester.

Great Massingham
East of King's Lynn, this picture postcard village has a number of attractive large ponds. These were used as fishponds by the 11th-century Augustinian abbey which once stood here.

Lavender farm England's oldest lavender farm is at Caley Mill, between King's Lynn and Hunstanton. More than 150 varieties of lavender are cultivated here and the farm hosts a lavender festival each July when the crop is harvested. Right: the Cliff Parade bowls green at the seaside resort of Hunstanton.

Old Hunstanton Constructed in 1844, the Old Lighthouse is a prominent landmark in this picturesque village. The distinctive Hunstanton Cliffs (below) lie beyond the town's promenade and are a magnet for fossil-hunters.

Heacham Situated between King's Lynn and Hunstanton, Heacham has two beaches with panoramic views west across the Wash. This westerly aspect means that glorious sunsets can be enjoyed at Heacham.

Snettisham South of Hunstanton, Snettisham is a pretty village with spectacular views across the Wash towards Lincolnshire. In the depths of winter great flocks of geese can be seen commuting between their safe roosts in the Wash and nearby farmland.

Brancaster The three villages of Brancaster, Brancaster Staithe and Burnham Deepdale form a more or less continuous line along the marshland fringing Brancaster Bay. Legend has it that England's greatest naval commander, Lord Horatio Nelson, sailed his first boat at Brancaster Staithe (below). Nelson was born at nearby Burnham Thorpe where his father was the rector of All Saints Church.

The Tower Mill at Burnham Overy Staithe.

Blakeney Point The silting of the estuary at Blakeney has left a fascinating landscape of marshes, sand hills and mud banks, criss-crossed by creeks and narrow channels. The seal colony can be reached by boat.

Cley Mill The 18th-century windmill at Cley-next-the Sea stands at the edge of marshes.

Wells-next-the-Sea Despite its name, the town now stands about a mile from open water. It is packed with historic houses and narrow lanes, or "yards", lead down to the bustling quayside. The brightly coloured beach huts (below) are half a mile from the harbour.

Cromer Situated on a cliff-top overlooking fine sandy beaches, Cromer (right) is north Norfolk's premier seaside resort. The town's elegant Edwardian pier (left and below left) was one of the first "pleasure" piers to be built in the 20th century; it celebrated its centenary in 2001.

Sheringham Fishing was once the lifeblood of this attractive town (below); today at sunrise fishermen continue to push their boats out to sea from the gaps in the cliff known as "The Hythe".

How Hill The river Ant flows close to the Broadland village of Ludham. Nearby is How Hill House which is now a study centre. There are three restored windmills at How Hill including the evocative Turf Fen mill (left), erected in 1875 to drain Horning marshes into the river Ant, and a modern wind pump.

Hickling Broad With its traditional reed-thatched boat houses, the moorings at Hickling Broad by the Pleasure Boat Inn present an evocative Broadland scene – complete with a pretty village. Hickling Broad is the largest of the navigable lakes in the Broads, a watery region which straddles both Norfolk and Suffolk with over 200 miles of navigable rivers, dykes and cuts connecting more than 50 Broads.

Horsey Mill This fully restored drainage windpump stands proudly beside the edge of Horsey Mere between Sea Palling and Winterton-on-Sea.